Notes from an Aspergirl

Annabel Barker

BookLeaf Publishing

India | USA | UK

Presentation by *BookLeaf Publishing*

Web: www.bookleafpub.com

E-mail: info@bookleafpub.com

ISBN: 9789357696951

First edition 2023

A Thousand Things Before Thin

Things to aim for:
Compassion over curves
Sincerity over sexiness
Happiness over hips
Loyalty over lips
Brightness over big behind
Kindness over killer cheekbones
A thousand things before thin.

Things to be:
Polite over pretty
Wise over willowy
Diligent over delicate
Mindful over materialistic
Truthful over tinted
Understanding over underweight
A thousand things before thin.

Notes from an Aspergirl

I might seem young to be set in my ways
Though this is a result of my brain condition
You could say I have my own tradition
Like everyone else, I have good and bad days.
I will always respond to you if you are kind
Sometimes I shall pass as being neurotypical
As opposed to society's stereotypical
Image of someone with a disabled mind.
There are those who know I am clever
Which means they might forget my trouble
Seeing the world from outside my bubble
In which I would happily stay inside forever.
Worse are those who think I am a retard
When I am not – I just find life hard.

Notes from a Lonely Girl

I say what I mean and I mean what I say
Only that isn't a good thing to do
People notice me when they want to
Whether it be tomorrow or today.
With me, they are at their wits ends
Seeming to consider shyness a crime
They ask me what I do in my spare time
Let me think – I try to make and keep friends.
I always fret what it can be about me
That is so unlikeable, not worth knowing
I'm a plastic bag caught in the wind, blowing
That people neither cannot or will not see.
All I want is company, to get out of this mess
Is that too much to ask? Apparently, yes.

Magic Wand Wishes

If I had a magic wand,
I'd undo my regrets;
I'd edit many incidents;
I'd erase my upsets.

To be a fairy or a witch?
Either way, I could cast a spell,
Choose between helping others
With my magic, or unleashing hell.

If I had a magic wand,
I'd grow wings so I could fly,
Or render myself invisible,
So you couldn't see me cry.

If I had a magic wand;
I'd learn to read expressions;
I'd understand our social cues,
Thus prevent depressions.

If I had a magic wand,
I'd alter and reverse time,
Learn to read peoples' motives,
Which are now clear as grime.

If I had a magic wand,
I'd be crystal clear;
I'd make myself understood -
That I'd cherish dear.

Overload

My brain aches, my body shakes,
My head pounds underneath the unwelcome sounds.

My ears burn, my insides churn,
My mind hurts as my sense overexerts.

My eyes sting, I feel everything,
My heart thuds whenever the loudness floods.

My hands twist on either wrist,
My throat sears as I am swallowed by my fears.

Too Much Information

There is too much going
On here - I wish you would turn it
Off! Please turn it off.

My head is pounding
Underneath the
Constant and pointless
Hammering of noise.

I wish it would stop and
Never play again;
For all our sakes, please turn it
Off and keep it that way.
Remember that unlike yours,
My ears are burning
At the pointless volume
That is unnecessary.
I wish you would turn it
Off - please keep it off and
Never have it on again.

The World I Once Knew

I always used to see the milky way,
the whole galaxy, when night took over day;
only now smog keeps their visibility at bay
when will I see the milky way again?

I always used to breathe clean air
with not an ounce of toxicity anywhere;
now greenhouse gases emerge and flare -
when will I breathe clean air again?

Tigers always used to thrive in the east
as they were able to freely hunt and feast,
only rapid deforestation threatens the beast -
when will I see tigers thriving again?

Polar bears always used to roam on ice
as solid as snowy furniture, that would suffice
to support it, only it began to melt and deice -
when will I see polar bears on hard ice again?

I always used to swim in a clean sea,
where every kind of marine life was free
from oils and plastics the eye cannot see -
when will I swim in a clean sea again?

Once upon a time, Christmas was white,
as snow glowed and brightened the night,
glittering in both the sun and moonlight -
when will I have a white Christmas again?

Aspergirls

Some of us have straight hair,
Others have waves or curls;
Some of us are tomboys,
Others are girly girls.

Diverse like flowers and plants,
Our skins are black, brown and white;
No two of us are the same,
Our hair is dark, fair and light.

We live all over the world,
Coming in every shape and size;
Bearing every nationality with
Light, dark, big and small eyes.

There are creative minds
While some are academic;
It has always been like this -
Autism is not an epidemic.

An Autistic Mind

It's hard to understand how people think
Because my brain is wired a certain way.
Yet people fail to see me flail and sink
Beneath the rules of social games to play.
Confusion and cries for help don't go far,
Instead I'm expected to work things out;
So I watch intently from inside the jar
That keeps me in a social brownout.
There are some people who expect
To see outgoing perfection from me;
Tis exactly they who don't respect
How painfully hard that is to be
Always and forever looking in each eye
Of those I talk to - I'd rather die.

Broken Bird

The bullying begins in Year Nine,
That's when it happens first.
I report it and all seems fine,
But they've yet to do their worst.

In Year Ten, it slowly starts again.
Rows, taunts, a block on Facebook.
In Year Eleven, I want to stay in my den,
Just to avoid a cruel word or look.

They like bringing up past episodes
That I want to forget about.
I quickly crack under their goads,
Gasping and crying my eyes out.

I learn to live in fear and despair
Of what might happen next time.
Crippled with terror, I stay in a lair
Where my existence isn't a crime.

I have to have someone with me,
Just to get to classes, getting
Anywhere is Apollo 13 - I can see
Bullies ahead, enjoying my fretting.

Schoolwork no longer on my mind,
I can neither focus nor concentrate;
Someone only has to be unkind
To reduce me to a quivering state.

Sick with fear, the broken bird
Not only has damaged wings;
She stumbles with eyes blurred,
Her nerves like cobweb strings.

They never say why they hate me,
Or why they treat me like dirt;
I only know they want to punish me,
To get a thrill out of seeing me hurt.

Dear Bullies

Dear bullies,
I'm sorry for reporting you
Whenever you targeted me,
For having terrible anxiety
About what you'll say or do.

Dear bullies,
I'm sorry I don't always meet your eye
Whenever we've exchanged words,
Though I'd feel safer in elephant herds,
Seeing as you want to see me cry.

Dear bullies,
I'm sorry for ever insisting
That you were the bad guys,
Despite your cruelty and lies -
I'm sorry for ever existing.

Rollercoasters

Sometimes they're allies
Who want me to do well.
Sometimes they're bullies
Who want to give me hell.

They change their minds
Like models change clothes.
They change their tunes
Like radios change shows.

They ask me how I am
If they have a good day.
They shout and swear at me
If things don't go their way.

They're like rollercoasters -
Up, down, all over the place.
They wouldn't know stability
If it slapped them in the face.

They know I'm looking for
Kindness and sanity;
Am I asking for the moon?
No, just good humanity.

They're as safe and steady
As three-legged chairs;
Even and predictable
As the rides at fun fairs.

People Like You

People like you are hopeless, useless,
Only second class compared to us.
We shouldn't have to tolerate you,
You're not worth anyone's fuss.

People like you are worthless, helpless,
An embarrassment to us normal people.
You make us cringe, writhe, recoil, fume -
We wish you'd jump off a steeple.

People like you are stupid, obtuse,
Took thick to make small talk or take a joke.
You never understand social cues or rules,
You're dense as a yew, slow as an oak.

People like you are irksome, tiresome,
We might like you if you weren't so dumb.
People like us are important, big cheese,
Compared to you, you stupid little crumb.

The Mask

It's that time again. Leaving the house.
Time to put on the mask,
Hold together the mess of a human shell,
Keep yourself in like hot coffee in a flask.
Act like a normal person -
Camouflauge, copy, mimic, fit in -
Listen to what society has to say,
Pretend to understand its rules unwritten.

It's that time again. Coming home.
Time to remove the mask,
Release the pressure of a day's pretending,
Drain the cold coffee from the flask.
Call it a day feigning normality,
Put the facade back on the shelf,
Set it aside for the next day,
Because finally, for now, you can be yourself.

Anxiety

Am I good enough? Or am I
Not quite right? If you could
X-ray my mind, you would see how
Inadequate I feel, low confidence and
Extreme worrying in social situations;
Trying times with other people have
Yielded me to this fretting.

Autism

Assumptions that I am
Unintelligent are not
True, because in fact
I possess a great deal of
Sensitivity and thought;
More so, indeed, than some others.

PTSD

Plagued by flashbacks
Triggered by reminders
Saddened by regrets
Distressed by memories.

Planet Peril

Polar bears struggle on slush,
Sea levels rise and boil;
Turtles tangle in plastic,
Fish are coated in oil.

Forests shrink in the wash,
The air is stifled with gases;
Resources are often wasted,
By greedy, thoughtless masses.

Global warming's just a myth,
Animals are not dying out,
Just go home and relax -
There's nothing to worry about.

If things don't work on Earth,
There's always Planet B;
Where all life from birth
Is flourishing and free

The Fox and the Hounds

The fox wants to get on with her life,
She hopes one day to have cubs;
Thus she is sensible and snubs
Anyone who wishes to give her strife.

The hounds decide they hate the fox,
Rather than say why, they make a start
On their torments - the fox's heart
Begins to break as if dropped on rocks.

The fox curls up like a hedgehog,
Wishing she had spikes to scare away
Those who want to darken her day;
Soon her terror settles like a fog.

The hounds never need to be sent
After the fox, nor do they need teeth
To tear her to shreds, like a wreath
Of despair; hopeless and bent.

The fox wants to curl up and die,
Rather than be torn apart by cruel words
That make her eyes wet and blurred;
Why do the hounds want to see her cry?

The hounds mutter amongst themselves,
Sneering and jeering behind the fox's back,
Looking forward to watching her crack -
All the while laughing like Santa's elves.

The fox is forever hurt and confused
By the hounds' hatred and seeks answers
Behind the spite coming from the cancers
Whose words ensure her heart is bruised.

The hounds are gone from her life now,
Never to be seen or heard from again;
Still, the fox only feels safest in her den,
Even then keeping her head in a low bow.